'I love these books! The stories and illustrations are just beautiful.'

Penny Whelan, SENCO, Luton.

I Don't Want to be Me: Amelie's Walk

Meet Amelie, a girl who doesn't want to be who she is. As she ventures out on a walk one day, she comes across a tree, a flea, the sea, a pea and finally a bee – all simply being who they are. One by one, Amelie majestically attempts to become each character, but soon discovers how exhausting and painful it is trying to be anything other than yourself.

Full of enchanting illustrations and relatable characters, *I Don't Want to be Me*:

- supports emotional wellbeing through a greater sense of self–worth and self–acceptance
- helps children to discover alongside Amelie, that being yourself is enough
- ends with a mindful reflection to help children explore and be with their feelings.

This book is essential reading for teachers, parents, and anyone who wishes to help children feel heard, seen and accepted, just as they are.

Anita Kate Garai is a teacher, writer and mindful wellbeing consultant.

I Don't Want to be Me:
Amelie's Walk

Exploring Self-Acceptance

Anita Kate Garai

Illustrated by Pip Williams

Routledge
Taylor & Francis Group

LONDON AND NEW YORK

Cover illustration credit: © Pip Williams

Logo and 'bubbles' design © 2022 Liz Tui Morris, www.bolster.co.nz

First published 2023
by Routledge
4 Park Square, Milton Park, Abingdon, Oxon OX14 4RN

and by Routledge
605 Third Avenue, New York, NY 10158

Routledge is an imprint of the Taylor & Francis Group, an informa business

British Library Cataloguing-in-Publication Data
A catalogue record for this book is available from the British Library

Library of Congress Cataloging-in-Publication Data
Names: Garai, Anita Kate, author. | Williams, Pip (Illustrator), illustrator.
Title: I don't want to be me : Amelie's walk : exploring self-acceptance / Anita Kate Garai ; illustrated by Pip Williams.
Other titles: I do not want to be me
Description: New York, NY : Routledge, 2022.
Identifiers: LCCN 2021051862 (print) | LCCN 2021051863 (ebook) | ISBN 9781032233338 (pbk) | ISBN 9781003277583 (ebk)
Subjects: CYAC: Stories in rhyme. | Self-acceptance—Fiction. | LCGFT: Picture books. | Stories in rhyme.
Classification: LCC PZ7.1.G3665 Iah 2022 (print) | LCC PZ7.1.G3665 (ebook) | DDC [E]—dc23
LC record available at https://lccn.loc.gov/2021051862
LC ebook record available at https://lccn.loc.gov/2021051863

ISBN: 978-1-032-23333-8 (pbk)

ISBN: 978-1-003-27758-3 (ebk)

DOI: 10.4324/9781003277583

Typeset in Londrina
by Apex CoVantage, LLC

For Emma, Kai and Amelie

For Todd and Nate

'I don't want to be me,' I said miserably,

as I wandered sadly up to a tree.

'Well, I am me, I'm a tree you see.

A tree is just what I'm meant to be. Don't you agree?'

'Hmmm, maybe I could be a tree . . .'

'Well, let's see,' said the tree,

as kind as could be.

So I stood up straight, as straight as I could

and waved my arms, just as a tree should

till my fingers went stiff

and my legs felt weak

and my throat was dry

and it was hard to speak.

'No, a tree is **NOT** what I want to be . . .'

and so I kept on walking.

'I don't want to be me,' I said miserably,

as I sauntered gently up to a flea.

'Well, I am me. I'm a flea you see.

A flea is just what I'm meant to be.

Don't you agree?'

'Hmmm, maybe I could be a flea . . .'

'Well, let's see,' said the flea, as kind as could be.

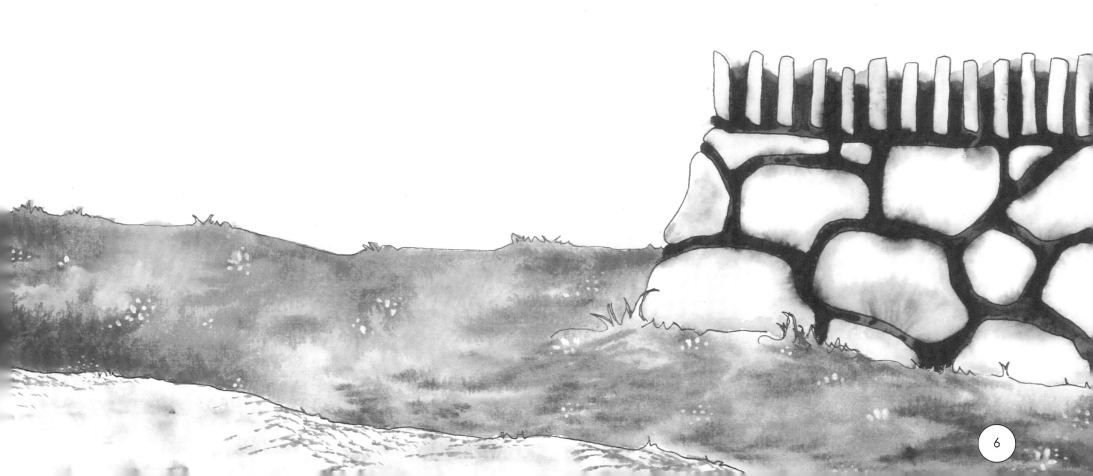

So I made myself extremely small
and hopped from a cat, to a dog, to a wall.

I kept on hopping for
days and days
until both my elbows
and knees were grazed.

'No, a flea is **NOT** what I want to be . . .'

and so I kept on walking.

'I don't want to be me,' I said miserably,

as I found myself standing by the sea.

'Well, I am me, I'm the sea you see.

The sea is just what I'm meant to be.

Don't you agree?'

'Hmmm, maybe I could be the sea . . .'

'Well, let's see,' said the sea as kind as could be.

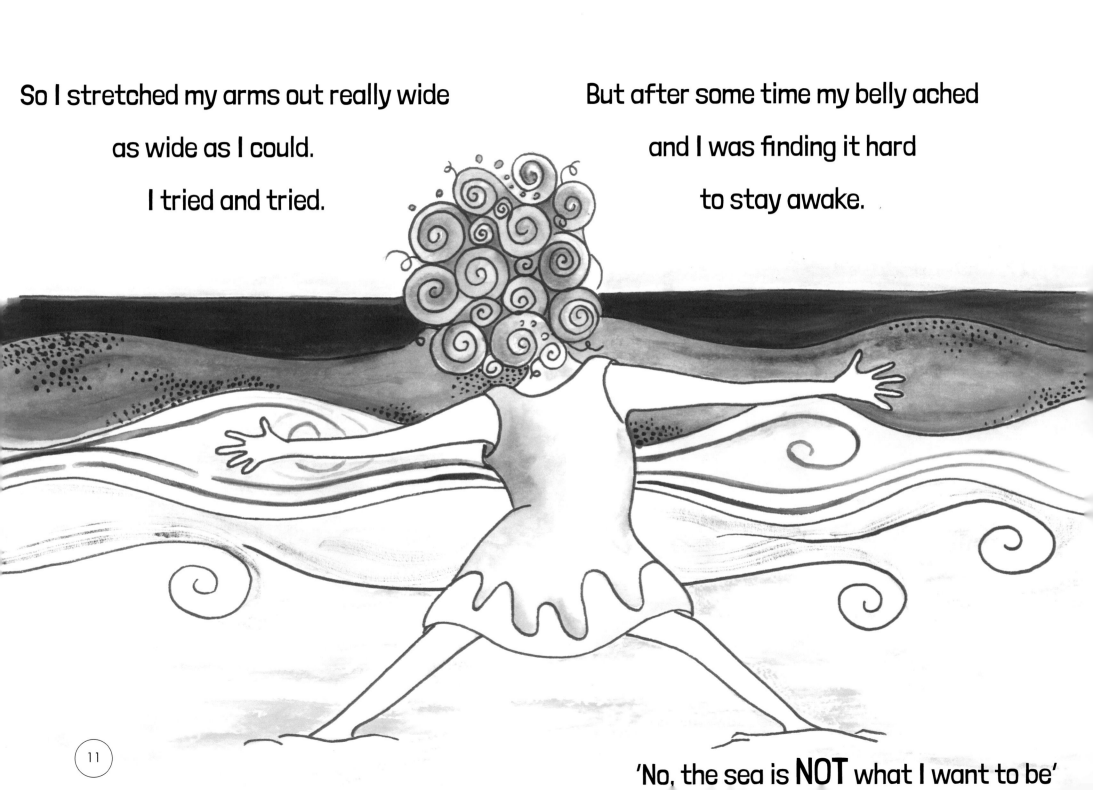

So I stretched my arms out really wide

as wide as I could.

I tried and tried.

But after some time my belly ached

and I was finding it hard

to stay awake.

11

'No, the sea is **NOT** what I want to be'

and so I kept on walking.

'I don't want to be me,' I said miserably,

as I looked at my plate and saw a pea.

'Well, I am me. I'm a pea you see.

A pea is just what I'm meant to be.

Don't you agree?'

'Hmmm, maybe I could be a pea . . .'

'Well, let's see,' said the pea, as kind as could be.

So I curled myself up really tight.

I tried and tried with all my might

until my back was aching and really jarred

and **UN**curling myself

was extremely hard.

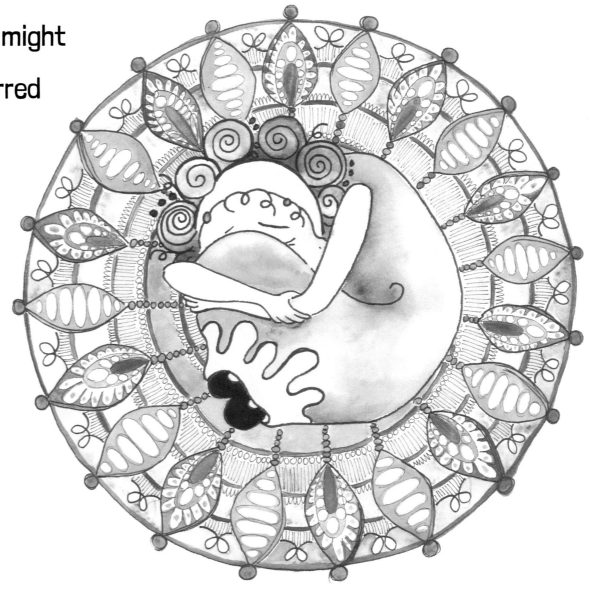

'No, a pea is **NOT** what I want to be . . .'

and so I kept on walking.

'I don't want to be me,' I said miserably,

as I sniffed at a flower and talked to a bee.

Well, I am me, I'm a bee you see.

A bee is just what I'm meant to be.

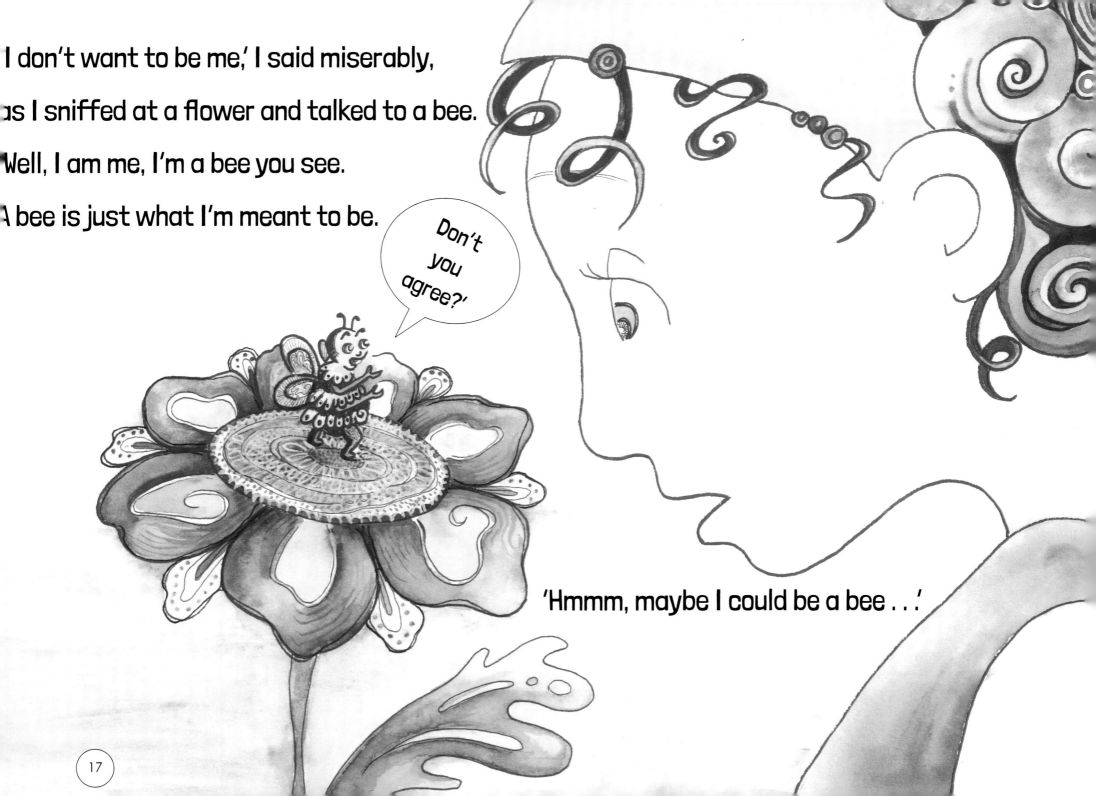

Don't you agree?'

'Hmmm, maybe I could be a bee . . .'

'Well, let's see,' said the bee, as kind as could be.

But by now my body couldn't take anymore.

I was so exhausted, that I flopped to the floor.

Then I let out an enormous sigh

as I lay on the ground and looked up at the sky.

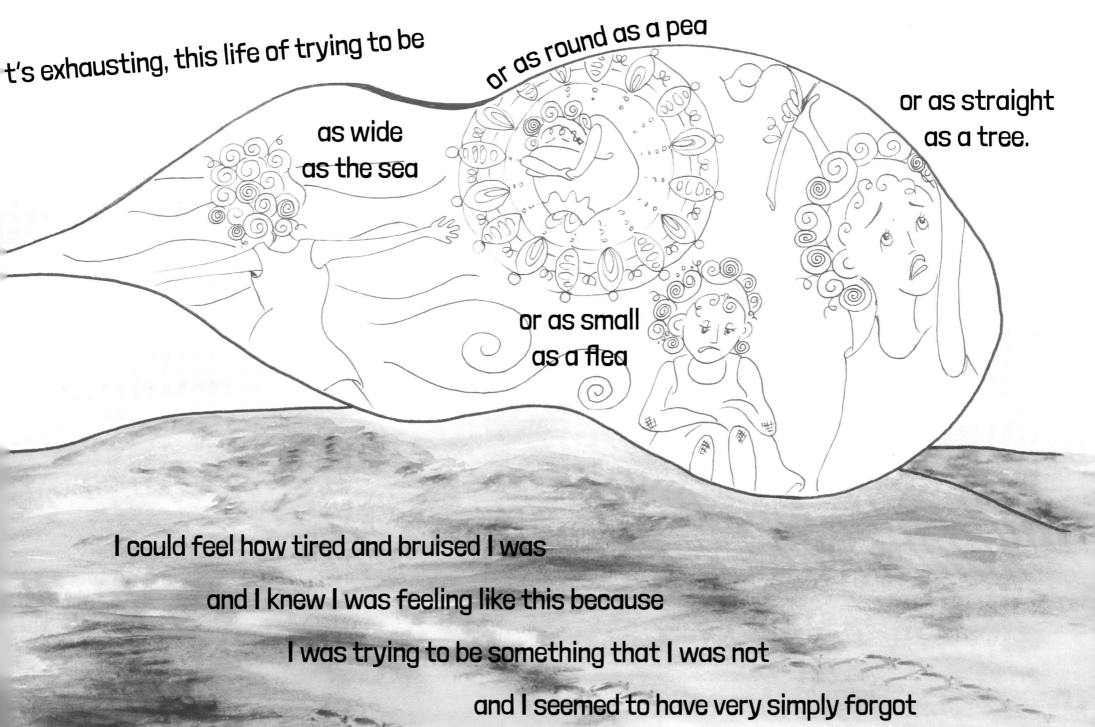

t's exhausting, this life of trying to be

or as round as a pea

as wide
as the sea

or as straight
as a tree.

or as small
as a flea

I could feel how tired and bruised I was

and I knew I was feeling like this because

I was trying to be something that I was not

and I seemed to have very simply forgot

20

hey, don't forget ME!

that just like the pea

and the tree

and the sea

(Hey, don't forget us!)

oops...

and the bee

and the flea,

Or ME!

I was just who I was meant to be...

Reflection

Have you ever felt like Amelie – that you don't want to be you?

What would this moment be like if you felt okay being exactly who you are?

As you reflect on these questions, notice how it feels in your body:

> Does the feeling have a colour?
>
> Does the feeling have a shape?
>
> Does the feeling have a movement?
>
> Does the feeling have a sound?

More reflections, activities and explorations are available in *Being With Our Feelings – A Mindful Approach to Wellbeing for Children: A Teaching Toolkit* by Anita Kate Garai (Routledge, 2022).

Printed in the UK by Severn, Gloucester on responsibly sourced paper